hjjnf   HEB
921 WEBB

Donohue, Moira Rose, author
Stompin' at the Savoy
33410017004013   02-13-2021

Hebron Public Library
201 W. Sigler Street
Hebron, IN 46341

STOMPIN' AT THE SAVOY

How Chick Webb Became the King of Drums

Moira Rose Donohue

Illustrated by
Laura Freeman

PUBLISHED BY SLEEPING BEAR PRESS™

To young William Henry "Chick" Webb,
all the world was a drum.

He tapped rhythms on iron railings.

Tinkety-tink!

He slapped rhythms
on marble steps.

**Thwapety-
thwap!**

He banged rhythms on garbage cans.

Boomedy-
boom!

And years later, on May 11, 1937,
he hammered them on his sparkly drum
set at Harlem's Savoy Ballroom in the
biggest band battle of the century.

William was born sometime in the early 1900s in East Baltimore, Maryland. He had challenges from the time he was very young. William had an illness that affected his spine. And one day, he had a bad accident.

He spied his grandmother coming down the street.

He raced down the stairs to see her and lost his footing.

Whomp.

He fell hard.

William needed an operation. Afterward, the family doctor told his mother to get a drum set to strengthen William's arms. But his mother couldn't afford drums— she couldn't even afford drumsticks!

So William made his own drumsticks.

He pounded sounds on pots and pans,
on floorboards and washboards.

Clangety-clang,
scritchedy-scratch!

William grew up with a hunched back. Kids called him "Chicken" because of the way he walked. Before long, his nickname became "Chick." He used it all his life.

Chick was nine or ten when he started selling newspapers. Before long, he was able to buy real drumsticks. If paper sales were slow, Chick beat out his music on whatever was nearby.

He twirled his drumsticks
and flipped them in the air.
People stopped to watch.
Sometimes they tossed
him spare change.

Chick saved his money
and bought a drum set.
Now Chick could
bang on the bass drum,
crash the cymbals,
and rattle the snare.

Dig-a-dig-a-dig-a-dig-a!

Chick stopped growing
at four feet, one inch—about the
height of an eight-year-old boy.
But being small didn't stop him
from making a giant sound.
He just needed a taller chair and
a higher bass pedal to do it.

Jazz music started in New Orleans, Louisiana. Soon, jazz bands were jamming all over the country. Chick was still a teenager when he was hired to play drums in a few bands. That's how he met the famous bandleader Duke Ellington. Duke saw how good Chick was and told him to start his own band. But Chick wasn't ready.

Then, in the late 1920s,
musicians started playing a new kind of
jazz music—a hotter music with a strong beat
that made people want to dance. This new music
was called swing. Chick had never had music lessons
and he couldn't read music. But he memorized
quickly and he practiced a lot. And his
heart beat in swing time.

This new music was just right for Chick. He decided to follow Duke's advice and form his own swing band. But Chick was a picky "bird." He wanted only the best musicians for his band. Once he found them, he and his band were touring the country. That's how Chick happened to hear about a girl with a satiny-smooth voice. Her name was Ella Fitzgerald. The moment Chick heard Ella, he hired her as the band's lead singer.

Being small didn't change the size of Chick's dreams.

"I got to get to the top," he said. And in 1937, he was almost there. He and his band played at the glamorous Savoy Ballroom on most nights. Some called him the "Savoy King."

Black musicians like Chick and his band were allowed to play at White clubs. But Black people weren't allowed to dance at White clubs. The Savoy was different. Everyone was welcome there.

Black and White people
who loved music tapped
their toes together.
Working-class people and
movie stars danced alongside
one another. People jumped and
jived to new dances all night long.
At the Savoy, the swinging never stopped.

In those days, live band competitions were the trend.
Chick loved band battles, probably because he almost always won!
But in February 1937, the little king lost to
Duke Ellington. Chick slipped off the bandstand.

"I can't take it," he said.
"This is the first time we've
ever really been washed out."

But Chick didn't let that stop him.
Benny Goodman's band was the biggest
of the big bands—number one in the country.
At over six feet tall, Benny was known as the "King of Swing."
Four-foot-one-inch-tall Chick challenged him to a battle of the bands.

Benny had some rules for the contest. The bands would play the same songs. Benny's band would play first. And on the bigger of the two bandstands at the Savoy.

Chick didn't mind. He knew his band could play on **any** bandstand. But could his band beat Benny's?

That night, four thousand people crowded together on the dance floor. Reporters from music magazines were there, too. The air shimmered and sizzled with electricity.

And outside the Savoy, on Lenox Avenue, another five thousand people jammed together, waiting to hear who won.

SAVOY

World's finest BALL ROOM

Backstage, Chick called his band together.

They towered over him, but he looked each band member in the eye.
"I don't want nobody to miss."

Benny's musicians took their places. They wore dark tuxedos.
The crowd pressed close to Benny's bandstand.
Benny raised his instrument to his mouth.
His clarinet crooned sweetly.
The crowd swayed.

Then Chick's band, in white tuxedos, took a turn.
Chick sat behind his sparkly drum set and held his drumsticks
over the snare drum, which was decorated with chicks.
He pounded his sticks. It was the same song—but
hotter and faster. **Swingier.**
The audience bounced
with the beat.

Back and forth the bands played. Songs like "Don't Be that Way" and "Stompin' at the Savoy." Gene Krupa was Benny's star drummer. That night, he played his drums so hard, he broke a drum head.

Finally, Chick's band played "Jam Session."
Chick pounded louder and faster
than a speeding train.
His hands were a blur.

Diggety-diggety-diggety-diggety-dig!

Benny's band just shook
their heads in disbelief.

Gene stood up and bowed his head to Chick.
"Chick Webb had cut me to ribbons," he said later.

Everyone there knew
that Chick had won.

Even the two rival music magazines gave
the win to Chick. And they gave Chick
a new nickname. From that night on,
he would be known as the

"King of
Drums."

More about Chick

Jazz music was born in New Orleans, but it had its roots in music from Africa and Europe. Swing music is a form of jazz. It's more rhythmic and less improvisational than early jazz music. In the late 1920s and early 1930s, big bands formed to play swing music. It was a music people wanted to dance to. New dances like the Charleston and the Lindy Hop became popular. One of the most famous songs Chick played, "Stompin' at the Savoy," refers to the foot stomping often used in some of these dances.

Chick had spinal tuberculosis and constant back pain for most of his life. In early 1939, his back pain worsened. He had surgery, but it didn't help. Chick found himself back in the hospital with further problems. On June 16, 1939, surrounded by family and friends, Chick sat up in his bed and said, "I'm sorry, but I gotta go." He fell back onto his pillow and died.

Sources differ about Chick's birth year (even though his grave marker says 1909). It was probably sometime between 1905 and 1909, making him younger than 35 years old when he died in 1939. At his funeral, Ella Fitzgerald sang "My Buddy." By the time she got to the end, she was weeping.

At just under five feet tall, the author understands that being short has its challenges. That's one thing that drew her to Chick's story—that, and having raised a percussionist daughter. While she cannot imagine the full effects of the suffering Chick faced in life, she felt a tremendous admiration for this man who overcame such difficulties to make incredible music.

To my brother-in-law, Dan, who shares my love of music,
and to my superlative sister, Deirdre!
—Moira

For my dad, who stomped at the Savoy too!
—Laura

Text Copyright © 2021 Moira Rose Donohue
Illustration Copyright © 2021 Laura Freeman
Design © 2021 Sleeping Bear Press

All rights reserved. No part of this book may be reproduced in any manner without the express
written consent of the publisher, except in the case of brief excerpts in critical reviews and articles.
All inquiries should be addressed to:

SLEEPING BEAR PRESS™

2395 South Huron Parkway, Suite 200
Ann Arbor, MI 48104
www.sleepingbearpress.com
© Sleeping Bear Press

Printed and bound in the United States.
10 9 8 7 6 5 4 3 2 1

Library of Congress Cataloging-in-Publication Data
Names: Donohue, Moira Rose, author. | Freeman, Laura (Illustrator) illustrator.
Title: Stompin' at the Savoy : how Chick Webb became the King of drums /
written by Moira Rose Donohue ; illustrated by Laura Freeman.
Other titles: Stomping at the Savoy
Description: Ann Arbor : Sleeping Bear Press, 2021. | Audience: Ages 6-10 |
Summary: "Black American jazz drummer William Henry "Chick" Webb led one of the big bands of
the swing era, earning him the nickname the "King of the Savoy.""-- Provided by publisher.
Identifiers: LCCN 2020031592 | ISBN 9781534110977 (hardcover)
Subjects: LCSH: Webb, Chick--Juvenile literature. | Jazz musicians--United
States--Juvenile literature. | Drummers (Musicians)--United States--Biography--Juvenile literature.
Classification: LCC ML3930.W33 D6 2021 | DDC 781.65092 [B]--dc23
LC record available at https://lccn.loc.gov/2020031592